A Look at Venus

A Look at
Venus

Ray Spangenburg and Kit Moser

Franklin Watts

A DIVISION OF SCHOLASTIC INC.
NEW YORK · TORONTO · LONDON · AUCKLAND
SYDNEY · MEXICO CITY · NEW DELHI · HONG KONG
DANBURY, CONNECTICUT

For
A N D R E A
and her prevailing spirit,
bright as the morning star

The photograph on the cover shows a view of the planet Venus. The photo opposite the title page shows an artist's view of the spacecraft *Magellan* surveying the planet Venus.

Library of Congress Cataloging-in-Publication Data

Spangenburg, Ray.
    A look at Venus / by Ray Spangenburg and Kit Moser.
        p. cm.—(Out of this world)
    Includes bibliographical references and index.
    ISBN 0-531-11765-0 (lib. bdg.) 0-531-16566-3 (pbk.)
      1. Venus (Planet)—Juvenile literature. [1. Venus (Planet)] I. Moser, Diane, 1944-
II. Title. III. Out of this world (Franklin Watts, inc.)

QB621 .S648   2001
532.42—dc 21   00-046245

Acknowledgments

To all those who have contributed to *A Look at Venus,* we would like to take this opportunity to say "thank you." Especially, a word of appreciation to our editor, Melissa Stewart, whose steady flow of creativity, energy, enthusiasm, and dedication have infused this entire series. We would also like to thank Sam Storch, Lecturer at the American Museum-Hayden Planetarium, who reviewed the manuscript and made many insightful suggestions. Also, to Tony Reichhardt and John Rhea, once our editors at the former *Space World* magazine, thanks for starting us out on the fascinating journey that we have taken—to Venus and many other places—during our years of writing about space.

Contents

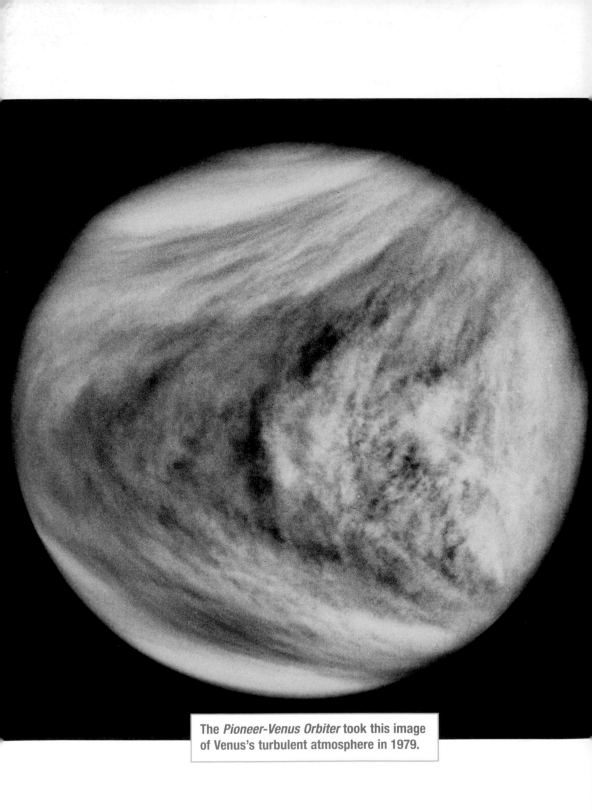

The *Pioneer-Venus Orbiter* took this image of Venus's turbulent atmosphere in 1979.

Taking a Hike on Maxwell Montes

Venus is one of the strangest worlds in the solar system. Its mysterious and eerie landmasses are completely veiled from Earth-based viewers by a thick covering of clouds. Nights on Venus are utterly black, unlit by starlight or moonlight. The stars are always hidden behind clouds, and Venus has no moon. Except for the occasional streaks of lightning that leap across the skies, the nighttime side of this world is bathed in total darkness. The atmosphere itself is poisonous to human beings. It is made mostly of carbon dioxide and has a thick layer of sulfuric acid clouds.

This view of the towering Maxwell Montes range was created on a computer using data gathered by *Magellan*.

A daytime visit to Maxwell Montes, a mountain range in the Ishtar Terra region of Venus, would reveal bright, filtered light from the Sun and a landscape much like some mountainous desert areas on Earth. The ground underfoot is similar to volcanic mountainsides on our planet. Yet, if you tried to go for a hike up these slopes, you would find the experience far different from a walk in the Adirondack Mountains.

The temperature would be searingly hot—as high as 900 degrees Fahrenheit (480 degrees Celsius). Even if a spacesuit could protect you from the heat, the going would still be rough. With an atmospheric pressure ninety times higher than the air pressure we are used to on Earth, moving around would be very difficult—something like trying to walk on the bottom of the Pacific Ocean.

The surface, though, is fascinating. Volcanic activity on Venus has created a variety of strangely shaped landforms. They look like crushed-in mountainsides, twisted spider legs, and stacks of pancakes.

This mysterious mound is an artist's conception of a lava dome on the surface of Venus. It is based on data supplied by *Magellan*, *Venera 13*, and *Venera 14*.

Large, continent-like land areas dominate the surface with volcanic mountains and high plateaus known as highlands. But no ocean waves crash onto the shores of these continents. Where Earth has vast regions covered with water, Venus has only hot, parched plains called lowlands.

Scientists have many probing questions about Venus. The atmosphere of Venus, the planet's extreme air pressure and heat, and the absence of water have all attracted keen interest. Why did this planet

An artist created this imaginary view of the terrain at the edge of a highland plateau on Venus. The details of the artwork are based on information scientists have about the continent-like plateaus Ishtar Terra and Aphrodite Terra.

develop so differently from our own? What warnings does Venus possibly hold for Earthlings? Could our planet become parched and poisonous like our neighbor?

This book explores the history of humankind's curiosity about and exploration of Venus. It describes what scientists have learned about our planetary neighbor and looks at what these discoveries can teach us about the past, present, and future of Earth.

Chapter 1

Earth's Neighboring Twin

Venus is the second brightest object in the nighttime sky. Only the moon is brighter. From Earth, you can see Venus shining brilliantly in the early morning—just before sunrise—or in the evening—just after sunset. From afar, it seems beautiful and flawless, moving in a nearly perfect circle as it orbits the Sun. Throughout history, the distant beauty of Venus has prompted many imaginative stories about the planet. At one time, some people envisioned this nearby world as a lush, green haven for space travelers—a place with babbling brooks and rich forests full of ferns and palm trees.

Venus (lower left) is the brightest object in the nighttime sky, except for the Moon (right).

Of all the planets in our solar system, Venus is—in many ways— most like Earth. To early astronomers, the resemblance seemed so striking that many described the two globes as "twin planets." The diameters of the two planets are nearly the same, their distances from the Sun are similar, and both planets have thick, cloudy atmospheres. Both planets also have large landmasses called "continents" that stand

Venus and Earth

Vital Statistics

	Venus	Earth
AVERAGE DISTANCE FROM THE SUN	67,232,364 miles (108,200,000 km)	92,955,808 miles (149,597,870 km)
DIAMETER AT THE EQUATOR	7,521 miles (12,104 km)	7,926 miles (12,756 km)
MASS	0.815	1.00
GRAVITY	0.91*	1.00
VOLUME	0.86	1.00
DENSITY	5.25	5.52
SURFACE TEMPERATURE	–47.2 to 932°F (–44 to 500°C)	–94 to 130°F (–69 to 54.4°C)
PERIOD OF REVOLUTION (LENGTH OF ONE YEAR)	224.7 Earth-days	365.24 Earth-days
PERIOD OF ROTATION (LENGTH OF ONE DAY)	243 Earth-days	1 Earth-day
MOONS	0	1

* If you multiply your weight by this number, you'll know how much you would weigh on Venus.

above the rest of the terrain. They each have mountains and plains and high plateaus too. Their *mass, gravity, volume,* and *density* are almost identical.

That, however, is where the resemblance ends. Scientists now know that Earth's most significant features are missing on Venus. Earth has vast oceans of water that lap the edges of its continents. Venus has no water at all on its surface, and no form of life exists on Venus. The atmosphere of Venus is entirely covered by clouds—not just the occasional thunderhead or swirling hurricane. Venus's clouds are not made of water vapor, and its atmosphere contains no oxygen.

The thick, butter-colored clouds that spread across Venus are composed of gases that would be poisonous to most living things on Earth.

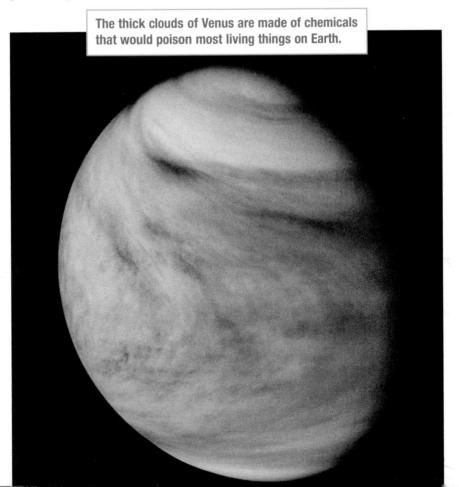

The thick clouds of Venus are made of chemicals that would poison most living things on Earth.

Venus's atmosphere is 98 percent carbon dioxide. On Earth, a delicate balance exists between plants, animals, and other living things. That balance makes life possible for all creatures.

In the process of growing, most plants "breathe out" oxygen while making use of carbon dioxide. Most animals, meanwhile, breathe in oxygen and give off carbon dioxide in the process of respiration. Thus, large quantities of oxygen and carbon dioxide are exchanged in a never-ending cycle. No such balance exists on Venus. In fact, many scientists think that no life has ever existed there. Of all the inner planets, Venus seems to be the most hostile to life.

Morning Star, Evening Star

For thousands of years, people didn't know these facts about Venus. They saw it glowing in the nighttime sky and were intrigued. Some ancient skywatchers kept track of Venus's movements. The Babylonians began recording their observations of Venus more than 3,600 years ago. Their name for Venus was Nindaranna. Other cultures had different names for this bright object that appeared in the morning and evening skies. The Assyrians called it Dil-bat or Dil-i-pat. To the Egyptians, it was the chosen star of Ishtar, mother of the gods. In China, it was named Jin xing. For the ancient Mayans, it represented the man-god Quetzalcoatl/Kukulkan. It was called Chak ek, the Great Star.

Because Venus travels so close to the Sun, some ancient observers thought they were looking at two different objects. Early in the evening—just after sunset—an especially bright spot sometimes glowed on the horizon. At other times, a similar bright object gleamed early in the morning—just before dawn. Early Greeks thought of them as the morning and evening stars. They called the morning star Hesperus. The evening star was named Phosphorus. To the Romans, this beautiful, bright, starlike object deserved a special name, and they called it Venus, after the Roman goddess of love.

So the planet Venus became a symbol of love—appearing at dusk or dawn to mark the start and finish of the romantic nighttime hours. Today, following the tradition begun by the Romans, most landforms on Venus are named after symbols of love and women. Continents bear the names of love goddesses—Ishtar Terra (after the Babylonian goddess of love) and Aphrodite Terra (after the Greek goddess of love). *Craters* and other features are named after famous women, such as Pavlova (a talented dancer), Sappho (the first renowned woman poet), Clara Barton (founder of the American Red Cross), and Gertrude Stein

Barton Crater was named after Clara Barton, the founder of the American Red Cross.

(a well-known writer of the 1930s). The only exception to the naming tradition is the mighty mountain range named Maxwell Montes.

Many of Venus's landforms were named during the twentieth century, and there's a good reason for that—the technology needed to detect, visualize, and observe Venus's surface features was not developed until the mid-1900s. Before that time, studies were confined to the general characteristics of the veiled planet.

During the fifteenth century, the Persian astronomer Ulugh Beg used a large *sextant* to make many careful measurements of Venus. The Danish astronomer Tycho Brahe included Venus in the many observations he made during the late sixteenth century. And in 1610, the great Italian astronomer Galileo Galilei made and used a telescope to study and describe the phases of Venus. His observations helped confirm the view held by the Polish scholar Nicolaus Copernicus that the Sun, not Earth, was at the center of the solar system. Copernicus had published his ideas in 1543, and Galileo became convinced by his own observations that Copernicus's idea—the heliocentric, or sun-centered, view—was correct.

Galileo reasoned that because Venus has phases like the Moon, the planet must pass between Earth and the Sun. Galileo also noticed that Venus appears smaller when it is full and larger when it is a crescent. These observations bolstered the claim that both Earth and Venus orbit the Sun. This worldview was completely out of step with the geocentric, or Earth-centered, view that had been held by European scientists and philosophers for centuries.

Copernicus's ideas seemed to diminish the importance of Earth and of humankind. The Roman Catholic Church considered this new view of the universe heretical, and church authorities forbade Galileo

The Astronomer-Prince: Ulugh Beg

Ulugh Beg or "great prince" was the name by which the Mongol prince Muhammad Taragay (1394–1449) was known. His grandfather was the famous conquering warlord, Tamerlane, also known as Timur, who led a Mongol tribe that lived in what is now Uzbekistan. Tamerlane made extensive military forays around the Mediterranean regions, and Ulugh Beg was born there. The capital of the realm, though, was in Samarkand, and it was there that his grandson eventually ruled. Tamerlane was feared for his extreme cruelty, but both his son and grandson are recognized for their development of culture. Ulugh Beg is best known for his scientific work.

At Samarkand, Ulugh Beg established a university. In 1424, he built an excellent, well-equipped astronomical observatory. Based on his own careful observations of the heavens, he created extremely accurate astronomical tables and star maps. Because he used Tadzhik, a language little known in Europe, his work did not become available to European astronomers until 1665. By that time, telescopes had been invented, and even more accurate observations had become possible.

Unfortunately, Ulugh Beg had no colleagues or students in his own land. When he was assassinated by his son in 1449, the tradition he had begun died with him. As a result, other scientists had little or no opportunity to learn from him. An important part of the scientific process—open communication—was frustrated by language, geography, and politics.

A statue of Muhammad Taragay, who was also known as Ulugh Beg

to promote the ideas of Copernicus. However, Galileo believed in speaking his mind. Eventually, he was tried by the Inquisition for the stand he took and was forced to recant. Legend has it, though, that as Galileo left the presence of the Inquisition authorities, he murmured, "And yet, it moves." Galileo was still convinced that he was right.

Galileo died in 1642. Amazingly, 350 years later, in 1992, Pope John Paul II announced that the Catholic Church publicly admitted that

Galileo had been unfairly persecuted for teaching his theory. At the time, the idea of a solar system with the Sun in the center seemed wrong to the church authorities and many other people. Now that scientists know much more about the universe, we can easily see that Galileo and Copernicus were right.

Chasing the Transit

Venus crosses between Earth and the Sun regularly, but not often—only about two times in a century. When that happens, observers can see a small, dark shadow floating across the Sun's disk.* In the 1700s, astronomers realized that they could learn a lot about the solar system by timing how long it takes Venus to move from one side of the Sun to the other.

* NEVER observe the Sun directly. Even though the Sun is far away, it can severely damage your eyes or blind you. Even fog, haze, or clouds will not protect your eyes. Always make indirect observations of the Sun. For example, you can project the Sun's light through a pinhole in a piece of cardboard onto a flat, smooth surface, such as a wall.

An English astronomer named Edmond Halley laid the groundwork for the first worldwide effort to measure this journey. He urged astronomers to organize into teams to time the trip, or *transit of Venus*, across the Sun's disk. By this time, astronomers knew the relative distances between objects in space. For example, they had calculated that Venus is about three-quarters as far from the Sun as Earth is. But they

Edmond Halley laid the groundwork for the first international observation of the transit of Venus.

had never been able to measure the exact distance between Earth and another object in the solar system.

Halley's idea was to place observers at a large number of carefully chosen sites around the world. Each position of observation had to be known exactly, and the beginning and ending of the transit had to be recorded precisely. Of course, the weather also had to cooperate, so Halley suggested that several teams should try to record the transit. That way, a cloudy sky in one location would not spoil the plan.

Halley's method had been used in 1672 to estimate the distance between Earth and Mars. But the transit of Venus could provide much more accurate results. The problem was that transits of Venus are very rare—two transits occur 8 years apart about once every 100 years. Halley presented his proposal to the Royal Society of London in 1716, when he was 60 years old. He knew he would not live to see the next transit, which would take place in 1761, but he was able to convince the Society to develop a plan that would make the great project possible.

The task of organizing this multinational undertaking fell to a French astronomer named Joseph-Nicolas DeLisle (1688–1768). DeLisle drew up a global map showing the regions of Earth from which the transit would be visible. Time was growing short, though. His map arrived at the Royal Society in London a little more than a year before the great moment, and much remained to be done. The teams would need instruments for navigating and measuring their positions exactly. They would need telescopes and clocks. They would need assistants to handle the equipment. And they would also need transportation to their assigned positions.

One British expedition sailed for St. Helena, an island in the South Atlantic Ocean. Unfortunately, clouds blocked the Sun and Venus, and no one on board the ship was able to record the transit. A second British team headed for Sumatra, which is now part of Indonesia. At the time, the French and the British were fighting the Seven Years' War (1757–1763). When the expedition had a confrontation with an unfriendly French ship, eleven crewmembers were killed, and the ship was so damaged that it had to return to Britain. The group was disheartened and frightened, but the Royal Society pressured the astronomers into sailing again. This time the scientists headed to the Cape of Good Hope, at the tip of Africa. The weather was good, and they recorded the only usable data from the Southern Hemisphere.

Halley had called for an international effort, so several French astronomers cooperated with the Royal Society—in spite of the war raging between France and Britain. The French staged four expeditions. The astronomers headed for a site 800 miles (1,287 kilometers) east of Madagascar in the Indian Ocean, a site along the coast of India on the Bay of Bengal, a site in Siberia in northern Russia, and a site in Vienna, Austria.

Although the French expeditions to the sites off Madagascar and India were headed into British territory, the scientists were assured by the British government that their ships would not be harmed. Nevertheless, British warships attacked both of the French vessels. As a result, neither expedition was able to make any observations.

Despite the efforts made by both French and British astronomers, the records of the transit were not as accurate or as plentiful as they had hoped. Based on the efforts of the observation teams, the distance between Earth and the Sun was judged to be anywhere from 77,846,110 miles (125,281,170 km) to 96,162,840 miles (154,759,090 km). Luckily, another chance to make additional observations was coming soon. The next transit of Venus would occur in 1769.

One scientist, a Russian astronomer named Mikhail Lomonosov (1711–1765), made a very important observation during the 1761 transit of Venus. He noticed a smudginess around Venus as it crossed the boundaries of the Sun's disk. As a result, he was the first to suggest that Venus has an atmosphere much thicker than Earth's.

Russian astronomer Mikhail Lomonosov discovered that Venus has an atmosphere.

More Observations of the Transit

Arrangements went a little more smoothly for the second transit of the 1700s. This time, the famous British explorer Captain James Cook led an expedition to Tahiti, an island located in what is now French Polynesia. The French government, impressed with the importance of the undertaking and its international nature, called off its warships and gave Captain Cook a clear right-of-way.

On June 3, 1769, everything went just as planned. The weather was clear and calm, the observers were organized, and many accurate meas-

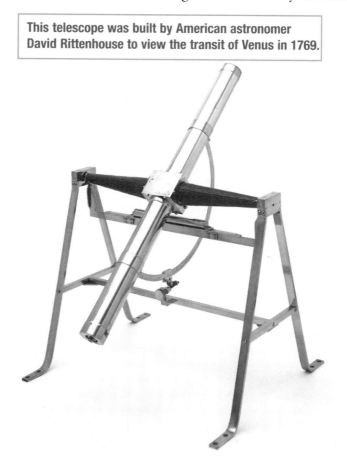

This telescope was built by American astronomer David Rittenhouse to view the transit of Venus in 1769.

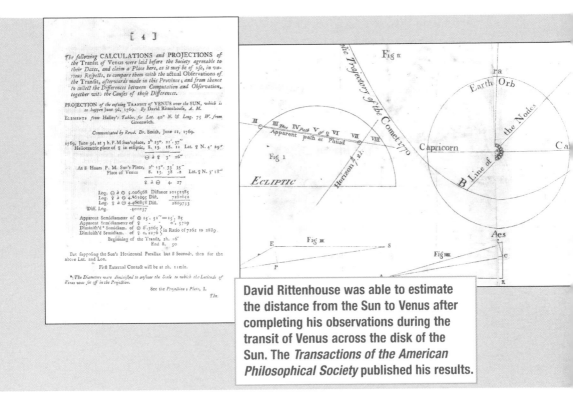

David Rittenhouse was able to estimate the distance from the Sun to Venus after completing his observations during the transit of Venus across the disk of the Sun. The *Transactions of the American Philosophical Society* published his results.

urements were recorded in Asia. Meanwhile, other teams made equally careful observations in North America and Europe. At last, a reasonably correct value for the distance from Earth to the Sun could be obtained. Using this information, astronomers could then calculate distances for all the objects in the solar system. International cooperation, carefully coordinated expeditions, and a little luck made the Venus transit observations of 1769 an outstanding success. Further adjustments would be made in later years, but basically, the big breakthrough had been achieved.

During the nineteenth century, Venus continued to attract a lot of attention. Prominent scientists such as British astronomer William Herschel and Italian astronomers Francesco Bianchini and Giovanni

Schiaparelli all took an interest in Venus. Again, in 1874 and 1882, astronomers had two opportunities to observe the Venus transit. Expeditions were organized with high hopes for obtaining even more accurate measurements than those of 1769.

However, even some records made by seasoned scientists standing side by side disagreed somewhat. Clear observation of this event was proving very difficult. Not only was it hard to get the teams of astronomers to the right place at the right time, but there was another problem. An optical illusion was making the job almost impossible. The disk of Venus seemed to cling to the boundary of the Sun's disk and then suddenly jump clear of it. How could anyone tell exactly when to start timing the planet's journey across the Sun's disk?

More accurate measurements would have to wait for more sophisticated instruments—and another era. Then the secrets of the solar system would begin to open up as they never had before.

Chapter 2

Visiting Venus

From the Babylonians to Galileo, and from Lomonosov to Schiaparelli, astronomers had discovered a lot about Venus. Yet they still could not see past the planet's thick, cloudy atmosphere. Even the invention of optical telescopes had not solved this problem. On Earth, clouds cover only about 40 percent of the surface, and breaks in the clouds allow people to see the landmasses and oceans clearly from space. Not so with Venus, however. Even the most powerful optical telescope cannot see through Venus's dense clouds. No one knew what the surface of Venus was like, or what the atmosphere was like below the cloud tops. Even as late as the mid-twentieth century, Earth's closest neighbor remained hidden and mysterious.

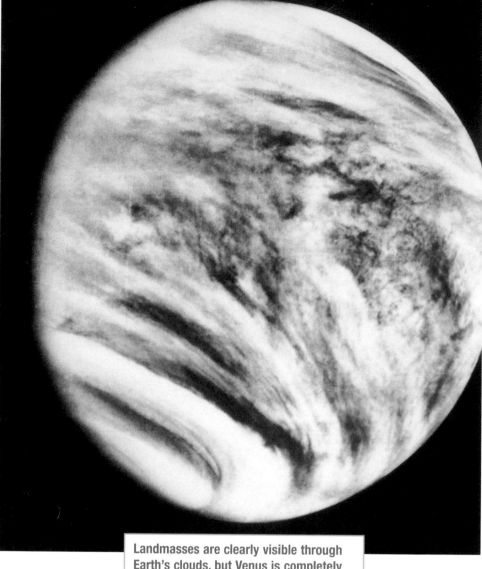

Landmasses are clearly visible through Earth's clouds, but Venus is completely shrouded by its thick, cloudy atmosphere.

The first breakthroughs began in 1958, when Earth-based radar observations began. At last, some idea of the land areas beneath the clouds began to emerge. However, the distance was so great that Earth-based instruments weren't powerful enough to give us much of an idea of what the surface was like. The concept was a good one, though, and it soon began to pay off.

Slowly Turning

One of the earliest mysteries astronomers puzzled over was a very basic question: How long is a day on Venus? For most objects in space, scientists figured out the answer to this question as soon as they had telescopes that could show a planet's features clearly. With Venus, though, the task was not so easy.

Early astronomers came up with figures, but no two observers agreed on the rate of rotation. The scientists didn't realize that they were looking at temporary cloud features—small white or dark spots that would appear in the cloud tops, remain for a few days, and then be gone. Until scientists could identify the planet's surface features, they could make no progress toward measuring the length of a day on Venus.

The second problem was that astronomers usually made their observations when Venus approached closest to Earth. However, Venus makes almost exactly five complete turns on its axis during the interval between its two closest approaches. So the same side of Venus always faces Earth at these times. Even radar was not much help with this confusing situation.

Finally, a breakthrough came in 1961. Using the 210-foot (64-meter) radio telescope at Goldstone, California, in the Mojave Desert, scientists were able to bounce signals off Venus and detect its surface features. This allowed them to time Venus's rotation precisely. Also, they saw how the strangely synchronized movements of Earth and Venus worked to bring the same features back again, time after time. Earth's twin, they had discovered, rotates very slowly. It takes Venus 243 Earth-days to turn once on its axis. It takes a bit less time—224.7 days—for Venus to revolve, or travel once around the Sun. This means that Venus's year is shorter than one day on that planet!

NASA uses a team of antennae like this one at the Deep Space Network at Goldstone, California, to track missions to Venus and other planets.

In 1962, a group of scientists discovered another interesting fact. Venus does not rotate in the same direction as the other planets. Instead of rotating in a west-to-east direction on its axis, it has a *retrograde* rotation. It turns clockwise, from east to west. This observation was confirmed at Arecibo, Puerto Rico, in 1964, and it is one of Venus's mysteries. Some scientists suggest that early in the history of the solar system, a *meteoroid* or *asteroid* gave Venus a glancing blow as it careened by. Such a blow might have spun Venus around and started the planet on its east-west spin. However, no one knows for sure why the planet rotates "backward."

These discoveries answered some long-standing questions about Venus. But many scientists thought they could resolve many more questions if they could get their instruments closer to the mysterious veiled planet and its secrets. It wasn't long before they could do just that.

Getting There

A journey to Venus began to seem possible in 1957, when Earth's first artificial satellite entered orbit. Called *Sputnik 1*, the spacecraft was launched by the former Union of Soviet Socialist Republics (also known as the USSR or the Soviet Union). The Soviet Union's objective was to capture world respect for its intellectual strength and rocket power—and hence for its Communist government. It was a political move with resounding repercussions.

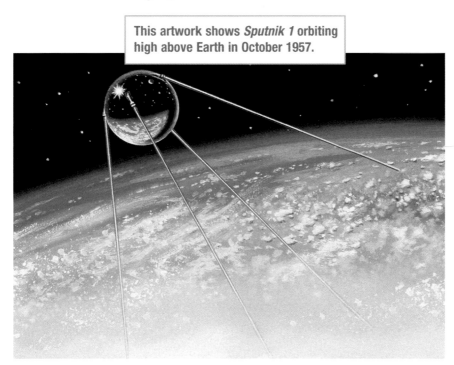

This artwork shows *Sputnik 1* orbiting high above Earth in October 1957.

Not wanting to be outdone by a political rival, the United States launched its own first satellite, *Explorer 1*, in January 1958. The "space race" had begun. Soon, both countries began sending a string of robotic spacecraft to other worlds. Mysterious Venus was high on their agenda. Everyone had questions about the veiled planet.

The first of many mechanical visitors to Venus zoomed into space on August 27, 1962. The spacecraft, named *Mariner 2*, had been designed and built by the United States. After its spectacular nighttime launch aboard a big Atlas-Centaur rocket, the spacecraft lifted into Earth orbit and then received a rocket boost that sent it toward Venus. It arrived safely at Venus about 4 months later and became the first successful mission to another planet.

Since that time, many more spacecraft have visited Venus and other objects in our solar system. Each one whizzes off to collect facts and pictures and then send them back to scientists waiting eagerly on Earth. Scientists are still learning new information about the planets from data collected by spacecraft more than 25 or 30 years ago, as well as by more recent missions.

First Cloud Close-Ups

On December 14, 1962, *Mariner 2* passed close enough to Venus to provide a glimpse of the cloud tops and a wealth of new information about the planet. The spacecraft's mission was the most basic type, a *flyby* that skimmed as close as it could to the planet and continued on out into endless space. *Mariner 2* came within 21,598 miles (34,759 km) of Venus—a little less than the distance around Earth at the equator. It sent some 65 million *bits* of data back to scientists.

An artist's impression of *Mariner 2* traveling through space

As it turns out, the data did include some hot news—both literally and figuratively. According to *Mariner 2*'s instruments, Venus is searingly hot—with a temperature reading of about 800°F (427°C) at the surface. Scientists were amazed. No one had expected such high temperatures.

Mariner 2 showed no breaks in the cloud cover, so glimpses of the Venusian surface would have to wait for another mission. The little spacecraft also found no indication of water in the atmosphere—although very small amounts were discovered later. *Mariner 2* also established that Venus does not have a *magnetic field* or *radiation belts* similar to Earth's.

Nearly 4 years later, another Mariner spacecraft took an even closer look at Venus. *Mariner 5* was originally a backup system for a voyage to Mars. Since it wasn't needed for that mission, NASA retooled it a bit, and on June 14, 1967, *Mariner 5* headed for Venus. It arrived on October 19 and flew much closer than *Mariner 2*—within 2,480 miles (3,991 km) of the planet.

Technology at Work: Powering a Spacecraft

Where does a spacecraft get its power? Rocket engines provide the power that lifts a spacecraft from Earth's surface, allows it to overcome Earth's gravity, and places it in orbit around Earth. Rocket power also gives an interplanetary spacecraft, such as the Mariner spacecraft, the initial push toward its destination. Once the vehicle is in space, ground crews may fire onboard rocket thrusters to adjust the spacecraft's *trajectory*, or path. But what runs the many instruments on board a spacecraft and the computer that receives instructions from Earth?

The energy for most of these activities comes directly from the Sun. It is collected by solar cells arranged in groups called solar panels, or solar arrays. They look like big, flat windmill blades or wings.

Within a solar cell, solar energy is converted directly into electricity. This process is called the *photovoltaic* effect. Since Bell Laboratories first developed solar cells in the 1950s, single solar cells have been commonly used to power calculators and wristwatches. They have also powered equipment in remote areas on Earth where it would be difficult and costly to use electrical cables or wires. Aboard spacecraft, engineers first used solar arrays to power *Explorer 1*—the first U.S. satellite launched in 1958. Spacecraft have been using them ever since.

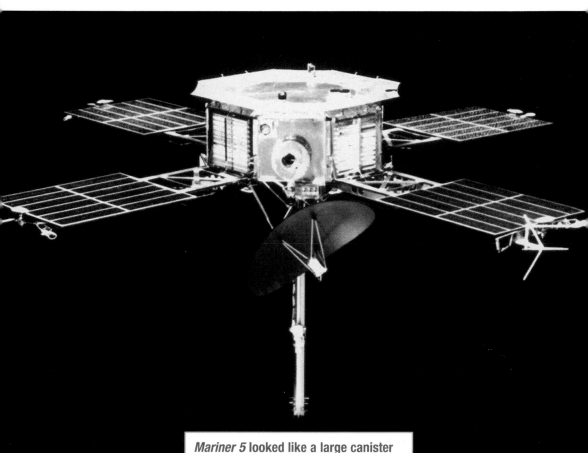

Mariner 5 looked like a large canister surrounded by the blades of a windmill.

Mariner 5 looked like a windmill attached to a big canister, with its four solar panels reaching out from the center. The canister-shaped part carried an assortment of precision instruments that were much more sensitive than those on board *Mariner 2*. *Mariner 5* had a central computer that managed the rest of the spacecraft's computer systems. Its instruments could examine Venus's atmosphere with radio waves and study solar particles—ions that stream out from the Sun.

The Soviet Union sent *Venera 1* to Venus in 1961.

Dodging Through Clouds and Landing

Meanwhile the Soviet Union had also found Venus intriguing. The Soviets launched their first attempt at a Venus flyby on February 12, 1961—18 months before the U.S. launch of *Mariner 2*. Unfortunately, the spacecraft, *Venera 1*, lost radio contact when it was 4.7 million miles (7.56 million km) from Earth. The spacecraft flew within 62,013 miles (99,800 km) of Venus, but its reports never reached Earth. *Venera 1* has continued to orbit the Sun ever since.

Several other Soviet missions followed, but launching spacecraft, tracking them, and making sure that their instruments will work at such enormous distances is tricky. It requires luck as well as expertise. Everything that could go wrong did go wrong for the Soviets. Several launches fizzled. Some spacecraft that launched smoothly failed to send back data. In March 1966, *Venera 3* accidentally crashed into Venus. It became the first spacecraft to reach a planet's surface, but it did not send back any data. Finally, though, *Venera 4* was launched successfully just 2 days before the United States sent *Mariner 5* into space.

Venera 4 arrived at Venus on October 18, 1967. It was the first planetary probe to be placed directly into the Venusian atmosphere. The equipment on board collected data and sent scientists on Earth the first on-site information about the atmosphere's composition, temperature, and pressure. *Venera 4* was not designed to reach the surface of Venus, though. The planet's enormous atmospheric pressure crushed the spacecraft before it could touch down.

Designing a spacecraft that could land on Venus was no easy task. Yet the Soviet engineers took on that job again and again. Each new design improved features that allowed it to dip farther and farther into

This is how the identical spacecraft *Venera 5* and *6* looked shortly before traveling to the launch pad.

the atmosphere. *Venera 5* and *Venera 6* confirmed and refined information about Venus's atmosphere. *Venera 5* came within 16.2 miles (26 km) of the surface, and *Venera 6* was only 6.8 miles (11 km) from the surface when it was destroyed.

These early missions were very exciting. They provided the first close-up views of Venus's cloud tops and the first on-site data of its atmosphere. Scientists now knew that planetary exploration could pay off with vast amounts of new information.

Golden Age: The Beginning

By the 1970s, both the United States and the Soviet Union had developed more reliable spacecraft designs, and seven spacecraft arrived at the mysterious veiled planet during that decade. The Soviets sent four of them—*Venera 7, 8, 9,* and *10.*

Venera 7, launched on August 17, 1970, became the first spacecraft to land on the surface of another planet. It touched down on Venus on December 15, 1970. Its designers had played it smart—the spacecraft arrived equipped for the planet's searing heat. It even had its own external cooling device. This equipment enabled *Venera 7* to survive on Venus for 23 minutes. During that time, it sent back priceless information about the planet's surface.

Two years later, another spacecraft arrived on Venus. *Venera 8* had two parts—a service module and a lander. After the service module released the lander, it burned up in the atmosphere. Meanwhile, a parachute helped slow the lander as it descended toward the surface. At the same time, a refrigeration unit switched on to protect the little lander from the immense heat on Venus's surface. As *Venera 8* whizzed through the clouds, it sent scientists information about the temperature, pressure, and the amount of light at various levels of Venus's atmosphere. *Venera 8* transmitted information about Venus for 53 minutes. During that time, the lander discovered that the surface of Venus was much darker than the surface of Earth.

By 1975, the Soviet Union had started sending missions of paired spacecraft to Venus. *Venera 9* was launched June 8, 1975, followed by *Venera 10* on June 14. Each of these spacecraft had two parts—an orbiter and a lander. They sped through space with their two parts bundled together. When the spacecraft arrived, the parts separated. The orbiter began its journeys around the planet, where it would relay the lander's signals to Earth. The lander, meanwhile, parachuted through the clouds, landed, and began its work.

Venera 9 separated on October 22 as it approached Venus. The orbiter immediately began its first voyage around the planet while the lander quickly plummeted to the surface to avoid heat buildup. Five

A model simulates the landing of the *Venera 9* spacecraft on the Venusian surface.

minutes after touching down on the surface, the lander began to send its first signals to Earth. Moments later, it transmitted a remarkable panoramic view of the area where it landed.

This was the first picture scientists had ever received of Venus from ground level! Now, at last, they could see what the surface of Venus looks like. The view seemed to be a steep slope—possibly the flank of a volcano—surrounded by rocks. A second view included the sky and horizon as well as several sharp, angular rocks as large as 3 feet (1 meter) across.

Three days later, *Venera 10* arrived at Venus. It separated into its parts—lander and orbiter—and the lander sped to its final destination. This time, the spacecraft seemed to touch down in a stony desert. Its pictures showed round, pancake-shaped rocks. Strewn debris from volcanic eruptions lay between the rocks, along with areas of cooled lava. Other spacecraft had shown that Mars and the Moon are covered with a layer of dust, but there was no evidence of dust on Venus.

The *Venera 9* and *10* orbiters each made more than a dozen revolutions. Their images of Venus's atmosphere were used to create the first large-scale pictures of the clouds that blanket Venus.

During the early 1970s, one other spacecraft ventured to Venus—*Mariner 10* from the United States. This was the last and most sophisticated of the Mariner missions, some of which had gone to Mars. *Mariner 10*, launched on November 3, 1973, became the first spacecraft to visit two planets. It looped around Venus and used that planet's gravitational field to continue on to Mercury—the innermost planet of the solar system. This technique, called a gravity assist, worked so well that engineers have used it many times on missions to other planets and to the Sun.

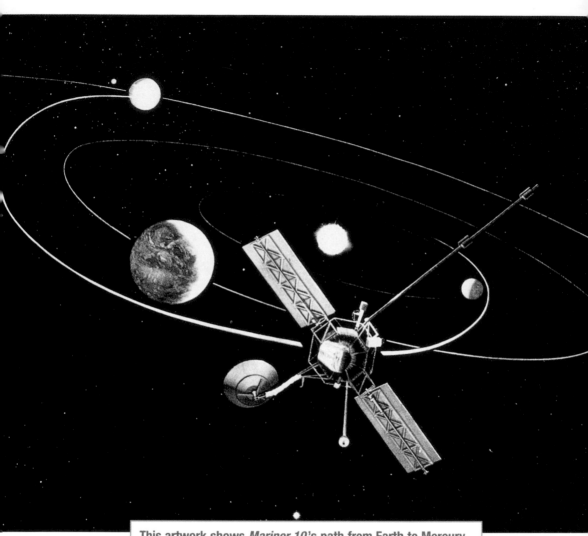

This artwork shows *Mariner 10*'s path from Earth to Mercury. On its way, the spacecraft received a gravity assist form Venus.

As *Mariner 10* whizzed within 3,585 miles (5,770 km) of Venus, it took a wealth of pictures. As a result, the world received its first ultraviolet images of the cloud tops of Venus.

Today, mighty rockets can fling a spacecraft off Earth's surface with tremendous speed—about 2.5 miles (4 km) per second. Yet even these powerful rockets do not provide enough speed to send a spacecraft on a really long voyage. Just about the only planets a spacecraft can visit with a straight rocket launch are Venus, Mars, and Jupiter. A simple rocket-powered mission launched to more distant planets might get there eventually—but the trip would take decades. So, when scientists and engineers want to speed up a spacecraft, they use a little trick.

Before the launch of *Mariner 10*, mission planners realized they could "borrow" energy from Venus's gravity field, and that's just what they did. Once *Mariner 10* had escaped Earth's gravity, the spacecraft became less and less influenced by the mass of its home planet. Soon, the Sun's giant mass exerted much more pull, and *Mariner 10* began orbiting the Sun instead of Earth. Then, as it swung by Venus, the veiled planet's mass tugged on the little spacecraft. But *Mariner 10* was traveling too fast to be caught in orbit around Venus. Instead, its path became bent as it flew by. Then an energy exchange took place between *Mariner 10* and Venus. As Mariner sped up in its new orbit around the Sun, Venus slowed down. However, because Venus was so much larger, it only slowed down a tiny bit. In fact, the slow-down was imperceptible. At the same time, *Mariner 10* gained a lot of speed.

Gravity assists have allowed visits to all the planets in our solar system—and spacecraft from Earth have succeeded in reaching the neighborhoods of all but Pluto. Rocket power lifting off from Earth only has to get the spacecraft to the first planet. Then, after getting a gravity assist, the rest of the voyage is "free."

Pioneers Head for Venus

On the heels of *Mariner 10*, the U.S. National Aeronautics and Space Agency (NASA) launched two more spacecraft. Unlike *Mariner 10*, the Pioneer Venus mission would focus all its attention on Venus. *Pioneer Venus 1* and *2* were launched a few months apart, on May 20 and August 8, 1978. *Pioneer Venus 2* arrived at Venus in mid-November, released four probes, and then descended with them into the atmosphere. One of the probes was a great success. As it descended, it sent a

This artwork shows the Pioneer Venus spacecraft at Venus. *Pioneer Venus 1* (right) orbited the planet and created a map of the surface, while *Pioneer Venus 2* (left) released four probes and then descended into the planet's atmosphere.

wealth of detailed information about the atmosphere to scientists on Earth. The probe survived the plunge to the surface and continued sending information for more than an hour.

Pioneer Venus 1 was the star of the mission, though. This stalwart spacecraft began orbiting Venus on December 4, 1978. Its main objective was to map the planet. After it finished this job, it continued to orbit Venus for another 13 years, sending back information all the while. *Pioneer Venus 1* finally crash-landed on the surface in 1992.

At last, planetary geologists could begin to piece together a picture of Venus's surface features. *Pioneer Venus 1* found a rift valley 3 miles (5 km) deep, 175 miles (282 km) wide, and 900 miles (1,448 km)

Technology at Work: Radar Mapping

In radar mapping, a transmitter on board a spacecraft sends out a microwave, or radar, signal. The signal bounces off the surface of the planet, and the spacecraft accurately records the time the bounced signal takes to return. When signals are sent in rapid succession, the results can be used to create a topographical map that shows depressions, peaks, valleys, plains, and plateaus.

This measurement of vertical elevation is called *altimetry*. A side-looking or forward-looking signal may also be transmitted from the spacecraft. This signal can measure the slope, or angle of incline, of a landform. This process is known as *clinometry*. Computers can then use these two kinds of measurements to produce color-corrected images that show what the feature looks like.

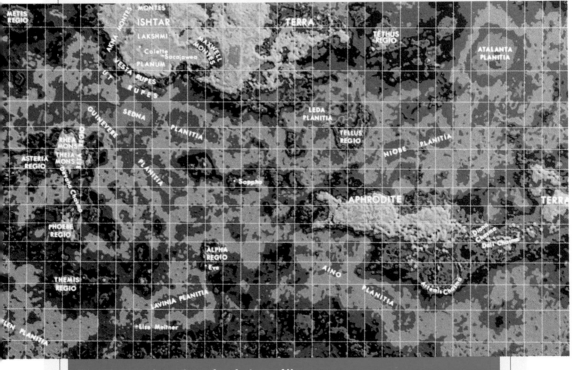

This radar map shows the surface features of Venus.

long. It also discovered a mountain ridge, Maxwell Montes, that rose 37,000 feet (11,277 m) above what would be "sea level" on Earth. That's about 8,000 feet (2,438 m) higher than Mount Everest, Earth's highest mountain.* Two more mountains jutted upward some 21,000 and 24,000 feet (6,401 and 7,315 m) above the surface.

More Drop-In Visits

After the grand success of the Pioneer Venus mission, exploration of Venus slowed down for a while. The government of the Soviet Union was having problems, and by 1989, it toppled. The United States also slowed its planetary explorations for several years. However, each country sent significant "drop-in" visitors to Venus between 1985 and 1990.

The twin Vega missions (*Vega 1* and *Vega 2*) were an international project launched by the Soviet Union in December 1984. Their primary goal was to get a close-up view of Halley's *Comet* as it sped near the Sun in 1985. Like *Mariner 10*, the Vega spacecraft looped by Venus for a gravity assist. They dropped off two probes that would release two 9-foot (3-m) balloons into the middle layer of Venus's atmosphere and two landers that would descend to the planet's surface.

Five years later, the United States launched a spacecraft named *Galileo* to explore Jupiter's four largest moons. The voyage would be long. At its minimum distance, Jupiter is more than 365,600,000 miles (588,400,000 km) from Earth. So *Galileo* began its journey by looping inward toward the Sun. It whizzed by Venus and then circled

* Unlike Earth, Venus has no sea level, so elevations on Venus are measured from the average radius of the planet—that is, an average of all surface distances from the center.

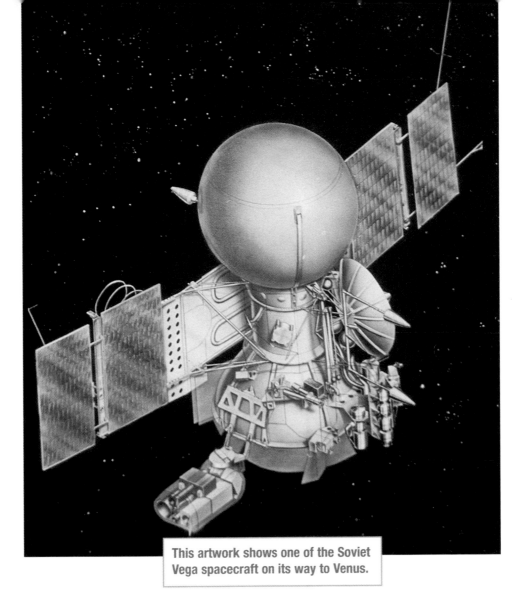

This artwork shows one of the Soviet Vega spacecraft on its way to Venus.

Earth twice, picking up gravity assists from both planets. Finally, it headed toward the outer solar system and Jupiter's moons.

As *Galileo* zoomed past Venus, scientists hoped to use the spacecraft's near-infrared mapping spectrometer (NIMS) to collect images of the dark side of the veiled planet. During *Galileo*'s trip to Venus, scientists got ready to turn on NIMS. But then they ran into trouble. Somehow, the equipment had overheated. Using computer signals,

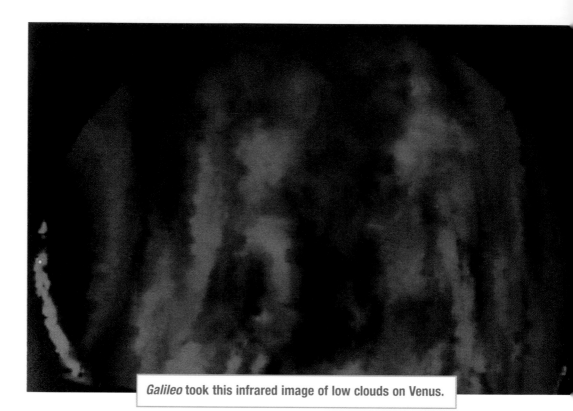

Galileo took this infrared image of low clouds on Venus.

scientists tried to cool the device. Meanwhile, time ticked away. Soon *Galileo* would no longer be close enough to have Venus in view. Finally, NIMS cooled off—just in the nick of time. Mission specialists opened up the instrument and were able to capture images of radiation escaping through the clouds in the planet's nighttime hemisphere.

Under these conditions, an optical photograph would appear completely black, but the NIMS images clearly showed heat leaking through Venus's thick clouds. They also showed cloud structures deep within the atmosphere—6 to 10 miles (10 to 16 km) below the cloud tops. NIMS was a stunning success at Venus.

Icing on the Cake

Without question, though, the most exciting and revealing mission to Venus was launched a few months before *Galileo* but reached Venus later. The spacecraft was named *Magellan*, after the Portuguese-born explorer Ferdinand Magellan whose ship was the first to sail around the world. The spacecraft's mission was to map as much as possible of the veiled planet by penetrating its clouds with radar. The approach was the same as for the Pioneer Venus spacecraft, but the equipment was much more sophisticated.

Magellan allowed scientists to study the geology of Venus in detail. The spacecraft used radar to penetrate the thick shroud of clouds around the planet.

Magellan, set out for Venus in May 1989 and arrived in December 1990. *Galileo* was launched in October 1989, a few months after *Magellan*, but it took just 4 months to reach Venus. How could that be? And why did *Galileo*—a mission to explore Jupiter and its moons in the outer solar system—go to Venus anyway? Wasn't that the wrong direction?

First, you need to remember that planets are moving targets. When *Galileo* was launched, Venus was in an ideal spot in its orbit to give *Galileo* the push it needed. When *Magellan* was launched, Venus was in a different part of its orbit. As a result, *Magellan* had to travel much farther to reach Venus.

These flight paths were not what mission planners originally had in mind for the two spacecraft. Both missions were delayed after the Space Shuttle *Challenger* disaster in January 1986, when a fiery explosion just after liftoff caused the death of its crew. *Galileo* was supposed to be launched from the Space Shuttle in May 1986. It would then use a powerful Centaur rocket to boost it straight for Jupiter. But the May 1986 shuttle flight never took place. NASA canceled all shuttle missions for many months while the *Challenger* accident was investigated.

In addition, key decision makers now felt that *Galileo*'s Centaur booster was too dangerous to travel aboard the Space Shuttle. *Galileo* mission planners had to be resourceful. Since *Galileo* was traveling farther than *Magellan* and needed a special trajectory, NASA engineers decided to give it *Magellan*'s October 1989 launch slot.

This meant it would take *Magellan* longer than planned to arrive at Venus, but the launch would require less energy and the spacecraft would be traveling at a slower, more manageable pace when it arrived. It could then move smoothly into orbit around the planet to begin its mapping mission.

Magellan's big antenna could send several thousand radar pulses each second through the clouds of Venus to the surface. It could map features as small as 400 feet (122 m) across and it could detect height differences as small as 100 feet (30 m). *Magellan*'s other goals included studying Venus's landforms, gathering data about processes related to impacts and impact craters, searching for evidence of erosion and deposits, examining chemical processes, and trying to understand the structure of the planet's interior.

The spacecraft would dip close to Venus, run its radar mapper for about 37 minutes, and then transmit the information back to Earth. *Magellan* succeeded in mapping 98 percent of Venus's surface. Based on the spacecraft's data, geologists learned that the planet's volcanoes held an important place in the planet's history, that Venus possesses unique features, and that the planet had no oceans. At last, scientists began to picture the lay of the land.

Chapter 3

Tortured Terrain

Beneath the dense atmospheric pressure and high temperatures at its surface, Venus's interior seems much like Earth's. It is composed of an iron *core* and has a semi-molten *mantle* just below the planet's rocky *crust*. And yet, even though Venus's interior structure is so similar to Earth's, Earth has a magnetic field and Venus doesn't. Why?

Some scientists think Venus probably lacks a molten metallic outer core like Earth's. An entirely stiff, dense core would explain why Venus has no magnetic field. Some scientists also contend that the veiled planet's extremely slow rotation may be partly responsible for the missing magnetism.

In many ways, Venus is nothing like Earth. Deep ocean waters cover much of Earth's surface. On Venus, there is no water. In fact,

Venus has more dry land area than any other planet in the solar system—much more than Earth. The many spacecraft missions to Venus have provided only a few photographs at ground level. Those images show a surface covered with platelike rocks—probably basaltic lava—interspersed with gravel and an occasional boulder.

Color photos from *Venera 13* and *Venera 14* show a deep butterscotch hue, accented with reddish-brown. However, the color doesn't show us what Venus really looks like. The planet's thick haze produces a false reddish hue.* Its atmosphere's thick layers absorb the shorter wavelengths as sunlight streams through. The surface of Venus is actually a dark, somber gray.

Forces within Venus's mantle have created hundreds of thousands of volcanoes on the planet's surface. Most of Venus's volcanoes are small—about 1 or 2 miles (1.6 or 3.2 km) across and only about 300

---

* In much the same way, we see reddish sunsets on Earth when the Sun sinks low on the horizon and shines through many layers of hazy atmosphere.

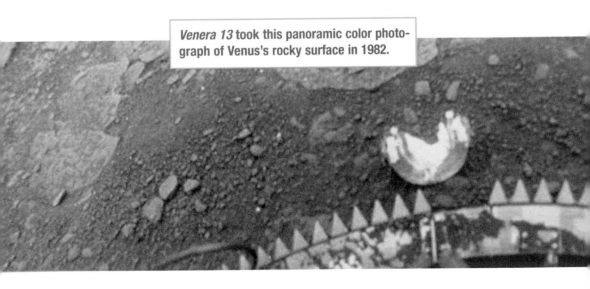

Venera 13 took this panoramic color photograph of Venus's rocky surface in 1982.

feet (100 m) high, but giant volcanoes tower above many of the planet's plateaus. Some rise higher than 35,000 feet (10,670 m) into the sky.

Magellan showed us that enormous lava flows have built up the slopes of these volcanoes. Around them the ground is broken by fis-

This computer-generated view of Maat Mons, the largest shield volcano on the planet Venus, was created using information gathered by *Magellan*.

sures, strewn with chaotic rubble, and pushed up by wrinkles and ridges. In some places, ridges, slopes, and cones have collapsed—probably from the tremendous weight of the lava. Scientists estimate that Venus's volcanoes and the lava that has flowed from them have shaped nearly 90 percent of the planet's surface.

That lava formed the gently rolling plains that cover much of Venus. For the most part, these plains rise or fall only about 3,000 feet (914 m). The radar maps created by Pioneer Venus showed scientists that about 20 percent of the Venusian surface is covered with plateau areas about the size of Australia. These highlands are not completely smooth though. They too have been shaped by volcanic action and are marred by fractures, cracks, and twisted landforms.

All this evidence reinforces the soil tests made by the Soviet Union's surface landers—which found more volcanic lava rocks than anything else. Venus, planetologists concluded, is a volcanic planet. Some scientists think that a few of Venus's volcanoes may still be active, but no one is completely sure. Does lava still spew from their cones or do they now stand dormant?

No Land on the Move

The extensive flat terrain of Venus tells scientists that little if any *plate tectonic* activity has taken place on the planet. On Earth, the surface, or crust, is broken into continent-sized slabs that are always moving. They move because the semi-molten *magma* that makes up Earth's mantle is always churning. Like the convection current that develops in a boiling pot of water, the hottest material at the bottom of the mantle rises and the cooler material near the top moves down to take its place. This giant cycle moves more than just magma, it moves the crustal plates that float on top.

In some places on Earth, the crustal plates move away from each other, and in other places, they collide. Where plates collide, tremendous pressure is exerted on the rocky material that makes up the plates. One of the results of plate tectonics is the formation of mountain ranges, such as the Himalayas. As the plate that includes India crashes into the plate that includes most of Europe and Asia, the land is compressed and pushed upward. The result is a series of huge folds that we call mountains.

There is little evidence of this kind of crumpling and shifting on Venus. Even though Venus has mountains, most appear to be volcanic in origin. Apparently, internal forces have not folded, pushed, or shoved Venus's crust. Although some sideways movement of the crust has caused minor compression and wrinkling, geologists believe that plate tectonics has not shaped the land on Venus.

Perfect Pockmarks

Venus is, however, marked by spectacular impact craters unlike any found on Earth—and many are perfectly preserved. Geologists have detected and named some 870 craters on Venus, including several as large as 168 miles (270 km) across. A few of these have stunning double rings. One of the most interesting craters, Barton

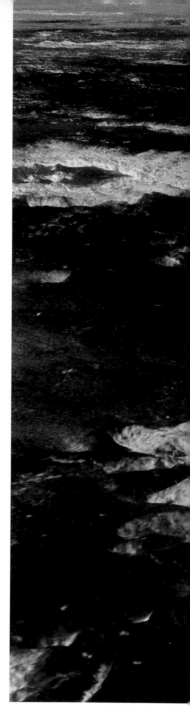

Howe Crater (center), Danilova Crater (left), and Aglaonice Crater (right) are located in the northwest region of Lavinia Planitia in Venus's southern hemisphere. This computer-generated representation of Venus's surface is based on data collected by *Magellan*.

Crater, consists of a ring of peaks surrounded by the crater rim. The crater's floor is paved with lava that once flowed up into the crater from deep inside the planet.

Venus's craters were formed when *meteorites* plowed into Venus's atmosphere at very high speeds—some 35,000 miles (56,327 km) per hour. Each one hit the ground with tremendous force that vaporized surface rock. Debris flew in every direction, leaving behind a cup-shaped hole surrounded by a rim. Midsized meteorites typically formed craters with a single peak in the middle. Larger meteorites often formed craters with double rings.

Some of Venus's craters are unlike those found on any other planet. Some have bright petal-like shapes around the rim. These "petals" consist of jumbled rock that was blasted out of the crater by the impact of the meteorite. Dark, circle-shaped craters tell scientists that some of the meteorites that entered Venus's dense atmosphere never hit the surface. They exploded in midair, but still left evidence behind on the ground.

No one was surprised by the existence of craters on Venus—all solid objects in the solar system have at least a few. Many worlds, such as Mercury and the Moon, are deeply pockmarked with countless craters upon craters caused by thousands of impacts. Some of these impacts date back billions of years.

As the solar system formed 4.5 billion years ago, all the planets, moons, and other objects in the solar system went through a period of major bombardment. Objects were battered, slammed, and collided like billiard balls. Chunks from one collision careened off into space and slammed into other objects. Sometimes the blow would be only a glancing hit, and sometimes bodies smashed and shattered. Sometimes they created huge gouges and scars, sometimes only tiny pits. Craters

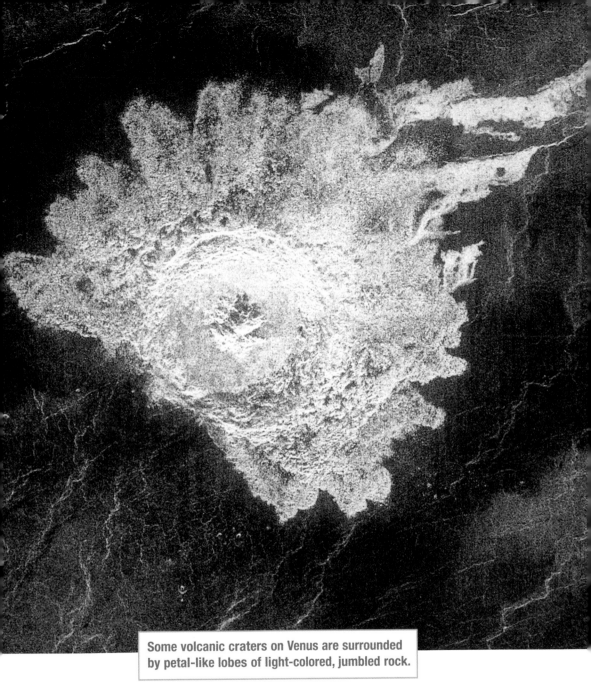

Some volcanic craters on Venus are surrounded by petal-like lobes of light-colored, jumbled rock.

of every size formed on the surfaces of all the planets and moons during this early period. Then, as planetary systems formed and orbits began to stabilize, the collisions began to slow down.

How the Solar System Formed

About 4.6 billion years ago, in the galaxy known as the Milky Way, a vast cloud of whirling dust and gas collapsed and condensed into a huge, flattened disk. At the center of this rapidly collapsing material, the temperatures became so high that fusion began to take place. Enormous energy and outward pressure increased steadily, and finally the contraction and condensation ceased. A star was born, and that star was our Sun.

Around the infant star swirled a huge, hot mass of gases and debris. This orbiting disk of material gradually cooled and condensed into masses of different sizes. These clumps were not big enough to form stars, so they condensed into *planetesimals*—the beginnings of what soon became the group of planets, moons, and asteroids that make up our solar system.

Initially, the planetesimals hurtled through space. When they collided, some shattered into a billion pieces. But others stuck together, forming larger objects. Eventually a few very large objects formed. Four terrestrial or Earth-like planets with rocky surfaces began to orbit close to the Sun. On these planets—Mercury, Venus, Earth, and Mars—most of the lighter gases, such as hydrogen and helium, were heated by the Sun and evaporated away. Farther away, material condensed into what planetary scientists call the "gas giants." Some of the remaining debris formed smaller bodies that began orbiting the planets. Material that was not swept up into the planetary systems—chunks of rock and ice that number in the trillions —became the asteroids, comets, and meteoroids that also orbit the Sun.

During the formation of our solar system, gases and rocky debris cooled and condensed to form solid masses that collided with one another, clumped together, and became planetesimals.

When you look at a close-up photo of the Moon, you can see thousands of craters—gaping gashes, medium-sized pockmarks, and tiny pinholes. On Venus, however, there are no small craters. In fact, Venus has no craters smaller than about 1.3 miles (2 km) across. Why? Scientists have figured out that small craters don't form on Venus because small meteorites never reach the planet's surface. They are destroyed as they fall through Venus's thick, high-pressure atmosphere. Long before they plow into the surface, they are crushed to powder. The Moon, on the other hand, has almost no atmosphere, so it has been struck by thousands of small objects.

Repaving with Lava

A few more things are odd about the craters on Venus. First, they are scattered randomly across the planet's surface. On most rocky surfaces in the solar system, erosion caused by regional storms or volcanic erup-tions smooths out some areas of the surface more than others. In those areas, fewer craters should appear.

Scientists would like to know why the craters on Venus are so evenly distributed. They would also like to know why there are so many large, undamaged craters. On a planet with as many volcanoes as Venus, scientists didn't expect to find so many craters that seem to remain unchanged.

On most rocky moons and planets, well-preserved craters are rare. On Earth, we seldom find big craters intact. Rains beat down on them, and rivers flow through them. The ridges that once formed the rim slowly wash away. Millions or billions of years after the impact, only the flat crater floor and a few jumbled rocks in a circular pattern remain.

Venus, of course, is different. There, no water pelts down from the sky. No rivers ramble across the surface. No oceans wash across the expanses of hot, desert rock. But Venus is a volcanic planet. Why hasn't flowing lava destroyed or marred the shape of more large craters?

Whenever volcanoes spew lava and bulges of magma ooze through the crust, the surface tends to lose the signs of its history. Lava smooths the surface. It fills ancient craters and gashes left by billions of years of

As lava flows out of Sif Mons and other volcanoes on Venus, the cratered surface is "repaved." Computer artists used data from *Magellan* to create this image.

colliding meteorites. Scientists call this process "repaving the surface." A "young" surface is one that has "new paving," or a "new skin," and few signs of age. An "old" surface is one that shows the history of billions of years of impacts.

By looking at a planet's craters, geologists can tell how long ago a surface was "repaved" by lava or erosion. First, they count the number of well-preserved craters in an area. Then they compare that number to the number of craters found on a surface where the age is known, such as an area on Earth or the Moon. For example, on the plains of central Canada, we see craters that are about a billion years old. On the Moon, we can see craters that are 4.5 billion years old.

When scientists compared the number of craters on Venus and Earth, they found that Venus is more heavily cratered. They estimate that the most recent "repaving" on Venus occurred about 500 million years ago—just about the time when complex life forms began to develop on our planet.

Based on these findings, many researchers think the entire lava surface of Venus formed at one time—in one cataclysmic event. According to this theory, an enormous amount of molten lava probably oozed out from the planet's mantle at one time and spread across the planet's surface. When this happened, most—or all—the craters that existed were wiped out, and craters that still exist today must have formed since that time.

However, some scientists do not completely agree with this idea. In a few areas on Venus, lava flows seem to have occurred more recently than 500 million years ago. So perhaps a few of Venus's volcanoes have been active since the earlier "cataclysmic event."

Hot Rocks and Bulging Magma

Scientists think that, from time to time, Venus's mantle may swell with upward-flowing currents called *mantle plumes*. In some cases, the plumes break through the surface and gush large quantities of lava. The lava may spread out into pools or lakes up to 15 miles (24 km) across, or it may flood the land and form vast lava plains or fields of small lava domes. Rivers of fast-moving lava may create enormous lava channels up to 3,728 miles (6,000 km) long. The lava may also pile up in layers to form huge *shield volcanoes*.

In other cases, mantle plumes do not explode through the surface. Instead, they scar the land, forming features called *coronas*. When the

This computer-enhanced view shows a corona on the surface of Venus.

molten material rises to the surface, it bulges up into a huge bubble and cracks the crust. Then small amounts of lava flow out and the center of the bulge sags, forming a shallow valley. When *Magellan* visited Venus, scientists got a close-up view of the planet's coronas. These structures, first noticed by Soviet scientists in the 1980s, range from 124 to 1,243 miles (200 to 2,000 km) across. While some coronas seem to be relatively recent, others are ancient. Thus, scientists believe that these strange structures have been part of Venus's geological history for a very long time.

Strange Landforms

Each mission to Venus has provided scientists with new information. Each has filled in more detail and added fresh clues. From the Mariner, Venera, and Pioneer Venus missions, scientists discovered that Venus is a sort of "pressure cooker," combining ferocious heat with enormous atmospheric pressure. These spacecraft taught astronomers about the corrosive acid in Venus's clouds and the high winds in its outer atmosphere.

More recent missions have provided even more information. Perhaps the most important mission of all, *Magellan* created detailed maps that finally gave scientists a nearly complete overview of the planet's *topography*. With its radar "eyes," *Magellan* collected the first comprehensive imagery of the structures beneath the planet's cloud cover.

The volcanoes on Venus have created a variety of unique surface features. These include "ticks" that formed when parts of a volcano's sides caved in. The result is a pattern of ridged marks that look like legs radiating from a rounded volcanic cone. From *Magellan,* the formation looked like a wood tick.

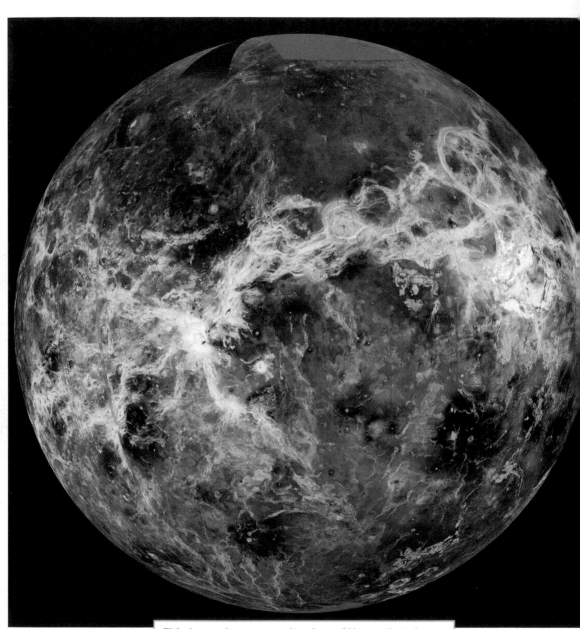

This image is a composite view of Venus that shows its topography. It was created with data provided by *Magellan*, *Pioneer*, and *Venera 13* and *14*.

Other volcanoes have lava flows that look like flower petals, extending into the area around the cone. Scientists call these "anemonae" (the plural of anemone), after the sea animals on Earth that look like flowers.

Still other volcanic domes show spidery arms stretching out from a center that looks like a cobweb. These structures are known as "arachnoids," which means spider-like structures. The spidery-looking webs connect shattered surface rocks like a network of cracks super-

Spidery volcanic structures called arachnoids stretch out wispy arms that connect cobwebby-looking centers.

imposed on circular shapes. From beneath, hot rock appears to be breaking through the round blobs and domes, causing the planet's crust to bulge, and the brittle rock to shatter and fragment.

Perhaps the strangest of *Magellan*'s discoveries was a type of structure found nowhere else in the solar system—huge, flattened domes that look like giant stacks of pancakes. Each pancake is some 15 miles (24 km) across, and the stack rises as much as 2,000 feet (610 m) into the sky. Some scientists think these "pancake domes" were formed by slowly oozing lava so stiff, thick, and sticky that it could not flow. Instead, the lava piled up and then gravity flattened it out. Other researchers have suggested that lava may have oozed up in several places along the length of a lava tube buried just beneath the planet's surface.

Slow Erosion

Erosion is a powerful force on the surface of Earth, but it is almost nonexistent on Venus. Venus has no rain, no raging rivers, and no crashing ocean waves. Nevertheless, images from *Magellan* do show some subtle signs of wind erosion. Although the wind at the surface of Venus is sluggish, one isolated volcano at the end of Parga Chasma shows signs of scattering caused by a steady northeast wind. Looking down from above, a wide, comet-like tail spreads brightly out from the volcano's cone. Scientists think that debris from the volcano has been spread by the prevailing wind in that region.

Other wind streaks are visible on the surface too. They fan out on the downwind side of various landforms. Unfortunately, the *Magellan* images are not detailed enough to show dust scattered by the wind. But scientists can see evidence that the wind has changed in some way because it was affected by the object it had to flow around.

An artist's impression of *Magellan* falling through the Venusian atmosphere at the end of its mission

Ellen Stofan's father worked for NASA, and she says she saw her first rocket launch when she was 3 years old. "The idea that we could explore the solar system, touch other worlds, was incredibly exciting," she later recalled.

When Stofan was a bit older, she became a rock hound and discovered a passion for geology. When Stofan realized she could combine her two passions by studying the rocks and geology of other planets, she knew what she wanted to do for the rest of her life. She earned a Ph.D. in planetary geology at Brown University, and she was on her way.

As deputy project scientist on the Magellan mission to Venus, she says, "I got to be present at 4:00 A.M. when the first Magellan images of Venus were processed. It was such an incredible feeling knowing that you are one of the first people to ever look at this area of a planetary surface."

When asked which planet she would like most to visit, her answer comes quickly: "I'd like to visit Venus. It's about the same size as Earth and has been affected by large volcanoes, mountain building, and quakes—just like Earth. These similarities may help us understand the same processes that affect us here on Earth. But it's extremely hot at the surface of Venus—more than 500°C, so I don't think my wish will come true!"

Planetary geologist Ellen Stofan (far left) joins colleagues at NASA's Mission Control.

There is also evidence of landslides on Venus—though not many. In a few places, masses of rock seem to have slid down a slope, turning end over end or rotating but not crumbling. Occasionally, researchers have also noticed scalloped edges on cliffs. These seem to indicate that material has slid away—and yet there is no sign of the resulting debris. Perhaps after the landslide occurred, a lava flow in the same area covered the fallen material. This explanation, while possible, is not completely satisfying to most scientists.

Interpreting images of Venus is difficult at best. Many of the planet's mysteries cannot be resolved until engineers develop more sophisticated imaging techniques.

Venus as a Fossil

Venus could turn out to be a geologist's paradise. On Earth, so much erosion and weathering take place that the planet's history is often hard to figure out. Geologists have to dig for ancient, untouched layers of sediment to find evidence that can help them figure out what Earth was like even a few thousand years ago.

On Venus, however, the surface is like a fossil. It shows scientists what the planet was like millions of years ago. The lava flows, volcanoes, and other features mapped by *Magellan* represent a fascinating and turbulent geology that stopped dead somewhere in time.

For some researchers, however, this situation is frustrating. They think there is a gap in Venus's geological history. Volcanic action and oozing lava do not seem to have continued into the present. Instead, these activities may have been confined to the first 90 percent of the planet's history. Geologists have no clues about what Venus was like between the time when volcanic activity seems to have ended and today. When scientists look at Venus, are they looking at a mimic of very early Earth? Or are they looking into Earth's future? If Earth's water disappears, will our planet become geologically inactive? Is that what happened on Venus? The cloudy veil of Venus has been pulled back, but many important questions about this planet remain unanswered.

Chapter 4

Lethal Air

The blank, bright bank of clouds that astronomers eagerly observed from Earth for hundreds of years did not prepare anyone for what scientists discovered about Venus's atmosphere in the twentieth century.

As you now know, the atmosphere of Venus is poisonous to most creatures on Earth. No living thing could survive there. Instead of the mixture of nitrogen and oxygen we have on Earth, the atmosphere on Venus is made up of carbon dioxide, and the planet's bright, yellow clouds are composed of sulfuric acid—the substance used in car batteries. A single drop of this hazardous chemical is enough to burn off your skin.

Venus's atmosphere is composed primarily of carbon dioxide, with clouds of sulfuric acid weeping overhead.

Weird Winds

At surface level, the atmosphere of Venus is calm, with only an occasional breeze. However, at the top of the clouds, the winds whip around the planet at a breakneck speed—205 miles (330 km) per hour. At this speed, air circulates around the planet once every 4 days.

When the exploratory balloons dropped by *Vega 1* and *2* investigated the middle ranges of Venus's clouds, they discovered some

Hydrogen-filled balloons similar to those used by Vega may prove to be the best method for exploring Venus's atmosphere.

strange vertical currents that are much more powerful than typhoons on Earth. These turbulent currents tossed the balloons up and down some 656 to 984 feet (200 to 300 m) at speeds of about 3.3 feet (1 m) per second.

Thermometers on board various spacecraft have shown that the cloud tops of Venus are quite cool—about 4°F (–15.6°C). Descending slightly toward the surface, more moderate temperatures prevail. Closer to the surface, the temperature spikes tremendously. At an altitude of 100,000 feet (30,450 m), the temperature reaches a sizzling 428°F (220°C).

From photos sent back to Earth by *Venera 9* and *10*, planetologists learned that at ground level, the view is relatively clear—much like an overcast day on Earth, not foggy as people had long imagined. The clouds are fairly high in the sky and a drizzle of sulfuric acid rain drips from them constantly.

Like drops of water tossed up and down in a gigantic thunderstorm cloud on Earth, particles in the Venusian clouds get bounced around a lot. As small particles of sulfur compounds condense out of the clouds high in the atmosphere, they start to form crystals. As long as the crystals stay in cooler regions near the top of the clouds, they grow larger and larger.

Eventually, the crystals develop into large, heavy droplets that fall toward the ground. Then updrafts in the clouds lift the droplets back up. This yo-yo action happens over and over. Finally, the deadly drops of sulfuric acid become large enough to drip from the lower surface of the clouds as acid rain. But, unlike rain on Earth, the acid drops on Venus never come close to the surface. In fact, they barely leave the clouds. The drops boil and then evaporate as they descend through the searing atmospheric heat.

Venus's Lessons for Earth

Some scientists think Venus may have been a vastly different place 4 billion years ago. Perhaps Earth was not the only "pale blue dot," as planetary scientist Carl Sagan once described our home planet. Perhaps Venus once had giant oceans, raging rivers, and gurgling brooks. Early in its history, Venus may have been cooler—cool enough for liquid water to exist on its surface.

Early astronomers saw evidence of Venus's mass of clouds without even knowing it. The planet's thick clouds reflect more sunlight than dark soil would, and that's why Venus is such a bright object in the sky. We now know that Venus's dense clouds cast a bright, hazy glow on the lands below. The probes from *Pioneer Venus 2* discovered that the atmosphere of Venus is slightly different below the clouds. It contains a tiny bit of water vapor and oxygen. Some scientists think the presence of even small amounts of these gases may mean that water once existed in large quantities on Venus. They believe that Venus may have had surface water when the planet first formed. Today, though, the planet is dry and hot.

Why is Venus's climate so much hotter than Earth's? It has a lot to do with the planet's position. Venus's orbit takes it 30 percent closer to the Sun. While that may not seem like a big difference, it's enough to account for some increase in temperature.

In fact, scientists have calculated that if Earth were just 10 percent closer to the Sun, its history would have been far different. The increased heat would have baked Earth's oceans, causing them to release tons of water vapor and carbon dioxide into the air. This change in the atmosphere's chemistry would have prevented heat from the Sun's rays from radiating back out into space and further warmed the planet.

This computer-generated view of Venus shows how scientists think the planet's sky and land look.

Today, the chemicals in Earth's atmosphere trap a small amount of heat. This process, known as the *greenhouse effect*, warms the lower atmosphere to about 60°F (16°C)—just the right temperature to support life. Without this mild warming, normal temperatures would plummet below freezing. In this way, Earth's atmosphere behaves like the glass windowpanes in a greenhouse. Despite this greenhouse effect, most of the heat energy that strikes the ground bounces back into space. This prevents our planet from getting too hot.

This artwork shows how the greenhouse effect works on Earth. Most of the incoming sunlight (yellow arrows) is reflected back into space, but some is absorbed by the atmosphere. As absorbed sunlight warms the planet's surface, heat energy is released as infrared radiation (red arrows). Although most of the infrared radiation drifts into space, carbon dioxide in the atmosphere prevents some infrared radiation from escaping. The trapped heat causes Earth's temperature to rise.

However, if Earth were a bit closer to the Sun and the atmosphere's greenhouse effect were more powerful, Earth would be substantially warmer. In fact, it might be similar to what we see on Venus today.

We know that both Earth and Venus are very hot deep inside. Radioactive material in the core of each planet gives off radiation that melts overlying rock and forms magma. The magma then pushes upward and bursts through weak spots in the crust, forming volcanoes. These volcanoes belch carbon dioxide into the atmosphere.

For million of years, the carbon dioxide from volcanoes on Earth was quickly dissolved in the waters of streams, rivers, lakes, and oceans. A mild carbonic acid formed, which then produced carbonate rocks on the sea floor. So, on our planet, most of the carbon dioxide remains tied up in the oceans and rocks.

Eventually, life developed on Earth. First there were only single-celled creatures, but soon more complex organisms evolved. Today, the life on Earth exists in complex ecosystems that continually recycle a variety of chemical substances.

Plants carry out photosynthesis. They combine carbon dioxide and water with energy from sunlight to form sugars and starches. When plant-eating animals munch on grasses and leaves, energy from the Sun and nutrients from the soil pass into the animals' bodies. When meat-eaters catch prey, the energy and nutrients are incorporated into the cells that make up their bodies. And when plants and animals die, their bodies are broken down by fungi and other decomposers.

Thus, the energy that fuels all life on Earth ultimately comes from the Sun. Without photosynthesis, life could not exist. But this process has another important job. It removes large quantities of carbon diox-

Green plants help keep Earth's atmosphere balanced by removing carbon dioxide from the air and adding oxygen.

ide from the air and adds oxygen. Less carbon dioxide means less global warming—a less powerful greenhouse effect.

Plants are not the only creatures on Earth that keep atmospheric levels of carbon dioxide in check. Tiny microscopic animals that live in the ocean use the carbonate materials in the ocean to build their protective shells. Thus, the life on our planet plays a major role in making it habitable. In other words, the evolution of life has helped make Earth a good place for living things.

On Venus, things were quite different. If oceans ever did exist, they quickly evaporated. Without the oceans, no liquid existed to dissolve carbon dioxide in the atmosphere. And while Venus and Earth probably started out with roughly equal amounts of carbon dioxide tied up within their rocks, most of the carbon dioxide on lifeless Venus eventually wound up in the atmosphere.

Because Venus's atmosphere contained significantly more carbon dioxide than Earth's atmosphere, Venus had a much more powerful greenhouse effect. There was no way for the sun's rays to escape into space—instead the heat was trapped in Venus's steadily warming atmosphere. Once we understand how Venus's out-of-control greenhouse effect operates, it is easy to see that if Earth had developed only a little differently, our planet's climate might be quite different today.

The lesson we can learn from this is that small changes can make a very big difference. That's why monitoring the changes human activities make in the environment is so important. We know that burning fossil fuels has already increased the levels of carbon dioxide in our planet's atmosphere. Automobiles and factories belch huge quantities of carbon dioxide into the air every day. Many scientists are concerned that our behavior may cause a more pronounced greenhouse effect on Earth.

On Venus, the combination of searing heat, a thick atmosphere of carbon dioxide, brutal acid clouds, and lightning blasts serves as an all-too-somber reminder of how easily our own climate could be damaged beyond repair. If we are not careful, Earth may one day be as unlivable as our mysterious neighbor is today.

Chapter 5

More Mysteries to Solve

Now that the ground-based radio telescopes and the Mariner, Venera, Vega, Pioneer Venus, Magellan, and Galileo missions have unveiled so much about Earth's strange neighbor, you may wonder whether any mysteries remain to be solved. The answer is, yes, there is still plenty for us to learn about Venus.

The most haunting overall question is: How could Venus and Earth have started out so similar and ended up so different? What does that mean for the formation of other Earth-like planets? Is Venus more typical, or is Earth? How precarious are the conditions we enjoy on Earth?

Galileo emerges from the cargo bay of the Space Shuttle *Atlantis*. It is one of the spacecraft that has helped us learn about Venus.

Scientists would also like to know much more about the internal dynamics of Venus. Does it still have volcanic activity? What is the composition of the planet itself? Does magma well up from within, and are new mantle plumes and volcanoes forming? If so, what kinds of gases do they belch into the atmosphere? Or is Venus now "dead" inside, like the Moon?

What would a closer look at Venus's landforms show us? What has happened to the surface of Venus over time? Why did resurfacing occur several hundred million years ago? What sort of chemical weathering attacks the surface? Why does the planet have a stiff outer shell instead of plates like Earth? Why does Venus have no magnetic field?

Did Venus's origin differ from Earth's in some major ways? Why does it rotate with a retrograde motion? Why does it have no moon?

What about the atmosphere? Why is it so thick? What effect have volcanoes had on its makeup and dynamics? Where did the strange layer of high sulfuric acid clouds come from? What chemical reactions are taking place in the atmosphere right now? Why do the clouds in the outer atmosphere speed wildly around the planet, in what scientists call "superrotation"?

Did liquid oceans, lakes, or even puddles exist at any time during the planet's history? Could life have developed there? If so, could any trace of primitive life forms remain fossilized in some ancient rock? And could we find them?

Planetary scientists are very curious about Venus. They would like to send additional missions to explore the veiled planet. They need more mechanical eyes, ears, and sensors on Venus—balloons that can float in the atmosphere and study it, landers that can test conditions

Someday spacecraft may once again land on the surface of Venus to explore its many remaining mysteries.

at ground level and take core samples, and orbiters that can take a closer overhead view.

So far, though, landers and atmospheric probes have not survived long there. The planet is brutally hard on spacecraft and none of the landers or atmospheric probes have lasted more than a few hours. Finding technologies that can overcome Venus's fearsome high-pressure, broiling, corrosive attacks on equipment is one of the big challenges for future missions. Until this is accomplished, we cannot perform studies over a span of time.

As scientists continue to study the worlds of our solar system, they constantly gain dramatic new insights about the universe. The more we learn about the history of our mysterious neighbor and "twin," the more we will discover about the past, present, and future of our own planet.

Vital Statistics

Spacecraft	Type of Mission	Year of Arrival	Sponsor
MARINER 2	Flyby	1962	U.S.
VENERA 4	Atmospheric probe	1967	USSR
MARINER 5	Flyby	1967	U.S.
VENERA 6	Atmospheric probe	1969	USSR
VENERA 7	Lander	1970	USSR
VENERA 8	Lander	1972	USSR
MARINER 10	Flyby	1974	U.S.
VENERA 9 AND *10*	Orbiter/landers	1975	USSR
PIONEER VENUS 1	Orbiter	1978	U.S.
PIONEER VENUS 2	Orbiter/probes	1978	U.S.
VENERA 13 AND *14*	Flyby/landers	1982	USSR
VENERA 15 AND *16*	Orbiters	1983	USSR
VEGA 1 AND *2*	Flyby, dropping two landers and two atmospheric balloons	1985	USSR
GALILEO	Flyby	1990	U.S.
MAGELLAN	Orbiter	1990	U.S.

Exploring Venus: A Timeline

385 B.C. — The Greek astronomer Heraclides proposed that Venus orbits the Sun, not Earth.

1610 — Galileo observes the phases of Venus.

1639 — English astronomers Jeremiah Horrocks and William Crabtree become the first to observe a transit of Venus.

1666 — Giovanni Domenico Cassini makes the first effort to calculate the time Venus takes to spin on its axis.

1691 — English astronomer Edmund Halley shows how correct measurements for distances between objects in the solar system could be calculated from the transit of Venus.

1761 — France and Great Britain organize the first expeditions to observe the transit of Venus, suggested by Edmund Halley.

Russian astronomer Mikhail Lomonosov discovers that Venus has an atmosphere.

1769 — A second group of scientists observe a transit of Venus.

1824	— Based on measurements from the 1769 Venus transit, German astronomer Johann Franz Encke calculates that Earth is 95,000,000 miles (152,887,680 km) from the Sun.
1882	— Measurements made during the transit of Venus improve the accuracy of estimated distances between objects in the solar system.
1911	— Using spectral analysis, U.S. astronomer Vesto M. Slipher shows that Venus's rotation rate is much slower than Earth's.
1923	— First ultraviolet images taken of Venus's cloud structure.
1932	— Carbon dioxide is discovered in Venus's atmosphere.
1957	— The former Soviet Union launches the first artificial satellite, *Sputnik 1.*
1958	— The U.S. launches its first satellite, *Explorer 1.* Venus is observed using radar for the first time.

1959	— The Soviet Union's *Luna 1* probe to the Moon becomes the first spacecraft to leave Earth orbit.
1962	— *Mariner 2* becomes first spacecraft to fly by Venus.
1967	— The United States launches *Mariner 5* to fly by Venus.
	The Soviet Union's *Venera 4* arrives in Venus orbit.
1969	— The Soviet Union's *Venera 5* and *Venera 6* arrive at Venus.
1970	— The Soviet Union sends *Venera 7* to Venus. It transmits data for 23 minutes from the surface of the planet.
1972	— The Soviet Union's *Venera 8* sets out for a successful probe of Venus.
1974	— *Mariner 10* flies by Venus on its way to Mercury and takes the first ultraviolet images of Venus's cloud tops.
1975	— The Soviet Union's *Venera 9* and *Venera 10* orbiters and landers arrive at Venus.

1978 — U.S. *Pioneer Venus 1* sets out to orbit Venus in May and arrives in December.

U.S. *Pioneer Venus 2* sets out for Venus in August and arrives in November.

The Soviet Union's Venus explorations continue with *Venera 11* and *Venera 12*.

1982 — The first color pictures of the surface of Venus are transmitted by the Soviet Union's *Venera 13* and *Venera 14*.

1983 — *Venera 15* and *Venera 16* radar mappers image 25 percent of Venus with a resolution of 1 mile (1.6 km).

1985 — Two landers and two atmospheric balloons drop from international spacecraft *Vega 1* and *Vega 2* as they head toward Halley's Comet.

1990 — The United States spacecraft *Galileo* makes brief observations of Venus while getting a "gravity assist" on its way to Jupiter.

Magellan arrives at Venus and begins a highly successful mapping mission that lasts 4 years.

altimetry—a measurement of vertical elevation, or altitude

asteroid—a piece of rocky debris left over from the formation of the solar system. Most asteroids orbit the Sun in a belt between Mars and Jupiter.

bit—in computers, the abbreviation for binary digit, the smallest amount of binary data

clinometry—a measurement that shows a landscape feature's slope, or angle of incline

comet—a small ball of rock and ice that travels toward the sun in a long orbit that originates on the remote outer edge of the solar system

core—the innermost region of a planet or moon

corona—a land feature common in many of the plains regions of Venus. It is composed of nested rings and grooves and is caused by volcanic forces within the planet.

crater—a rimmed basin or depression on the surface of a planet or moon, caused by the impact of a meteorite

crust—the outer surface of a planet or moon

density—the amount of a substance in a given volume

flyby—a mission that takes a spacecraft past a planet to make observations, but doesn't involve orbiting or landing

gravity—the force that pulls things toward the center of a large object in space, such as a planet or moon

greenhouse effect—a natural warming process that occurs around a planet when heat from the Sun is absorbed by carbon dioxide in the atmosphere and remains trapped on the planet

magma—molten material found in the mantle layer of a planet or moon

magnetic field—the area surrounding a magnet that is affected by the magnet's attractive force. Some planets have magnetic properties and, therefore, have a magnetic field.

mantle—the region below the crust and above the core of a moon or planet

mantle plume—a hot, upward-flowing current in the mantle

mass—the amount of material in an object

meteorite—a particle of dust or rock that strikes the surface of a planet or moon

meteoroid—a rocky or metallic object of relatively small size, usually once part of a comet or asteroid

photovoltaic—describes the process of converting energy captured from the Sun into electricity

planetesimal—the precursor of a planet

plate tectonics—a geological process within a planet, such as Earth, that causes its crust to break into plates and move slowly over time

radiation belt—an area surrounding a planet, such as Earth, that interacts with particles from the Sun

retrograde—"backward," or in the opposite direction from the usual. Venus has a retrograde rotation.

sextant—an instrument used to measure distances. It is used in navigation and to observe the altitude of objects in space.

shield volcano—a volcano that resembles the curve of a domed shield. Its gentle slopes are built up by many lava flows.

topography—the surface features of a planet

trajectory—the path traveled by a spacecraft or other object through space

transit of Venus—the passage of the planet Venus between Earth and the Sun

volume—the amount of three-dimensional space occupied by an object

The news from space changes fast, so it's always a good idea to check the copyright date on books, CD-ROMs, and video tapes to make sure that you are getting up-to-date information. One good place to look for current information from NASA is U.S. government depository libraries. There are several in each state.

Books

Branley, Franklyn Mansfield. *Venus: Magellan Explores Our Twin Planet*. New York: HarperCollins Children's Books, 1994.

Campbell, Ann Jeanette. *The New York Public Library Amazing Space: A Book of Answers for Kids*. New York: John Wiley & Sons, 1997.

Dickinson, Terence. *Other Worlds: A Beginner's Guide to Planets and Moons*. Willowdale, Ontario: Firefly Books, 1995.

Gustafson, John. *Planets, Moons and Meteors*. New York: Julian Messner, 1992.

Hartmann, William K. and Don Miller. *The Grand Tour*. New York: Workman Publishing, 1993.

Simon, Seymour. *Venus*. New York: Mulberry, 1998.

Vogt, Gregory L. *The Solar System: Facts and Exploration*. Scientific American Sourcebooks. New York: Twenty-First Century Books, 1995.

CD-ROMs

Beyond Planet Earth, Discovery Channel School, P.O. Box 970, Oxon Hill, MD 20750-0970.

An interactive journey to the planets, including Venus. Includes video footage and more than 200 still photographs.

Venus Explorer for IBM, Andromeda Software, Inc., P.O. Box 605-N, Amherst, NY, 14226-0605.

http://www.andromedasoftware.com

Includes images of Venus's craters, channels, chasms, mountains, and volcanic domes, calderas, and coronas. Uses data from *Magellan* spacecraft.

Organizations and Online Sites

These organizations and online sites are good sources of information about Venus and the rest of the solar system. Many of the online sites listed below are NASA sites, with links to many other interesting sources of information about the solar system. You can also sign up to receive NASA news on many subjects via e-mail.

Astronomical Society of the Pacific
http://www.aspsky.org/
390 Ashton Avenue
San Francisco, CA 94112

The Astronomy Café

http://www2.ari.net/home/odenwald/cafe.html

This site answers questions and offers news and articles relating to astronomy and space. It is maintained by astronomer and NASA scientist Sten Odenwald.

Magellan Mission to Venus Home Page

http://www.jpl.nasa.gov/magellan/mgn.html

This site describes the details of the Magellan mission and has a multitude of images and animations of Venus.

NASA Ask a Space Scientist

http://image.gsfc.nasa.gov/poetry/ask/askmag.html#list

Take a look at the Interactive Page where NASA scientists answer your questions about astronomy, space, and space missions. The site also has access to archives and fact sheets.

NASA Newsroom

http://www.nasa.gov/newsinfo/newsroom.html

This site features NASA's latest press releases, status reports, and fact sheets. It includes a news archive with past reports and a search button for the NASA Web site. You can even sign up for e-mail versions of all NASA press releases.

The Nine Planets: A Multimedia Tour of the Solar System
http://www.seds.org/nineplanet/nineplanets/nineplanets.html
This site has excellent material on the planets, including Venus. It was created and is maintained by the Students for the Exploration and Development of Space, University of Arizona.

Planetary Missions
http://nssdc.gsfc.nasa.gov/planetary/projects.html
At this site, you'll find NASA links to all current and past missions. It's a one-stop shopping center to a wealth of information.

The Planetary Society
http://www.planetary.org/
65 North Catalina Avenue
Pasadena, CA 91106-2301

Sky Online
http://www.skypub.com
This is the Web site for *Sky and Telescope* magazine and other publications of Sky Publishing Corporation. You'll find a good weekly news section on general space and astronomy news. The site also has tips for amateur astronomers as well as a nice selection of links. A list of science museums, planetariums, and astronomy clubs organized by state can help you locate nearby places to visit.

"Venus Hypermap" Web Site

http://www.ess.ucla.edu/hypermap/Vmap/top.html#topo_map

Click anywhere on this colorful map of Venus to visit major landforms close up. The site also includes a glossary and descriptions of views from the Magellan and Pioneer Venus spacecraft maps.

Welcome to the Planets

http://pds.jpl.nasa.gov/planets/

This tour of the solar system has lots of pictures and information. The site was created and is maintained by the California Institute of Technology for NASA/Jet Propulsion Laboratory.

Windows to the Universe

http://windows.ivv.nasa.gov/

This NASA site, developed by the University of Michigan, includes sections on "Our Planet," "Our Solar System," "Space Missions," and "Kids' Space." Choose from presentation levels of beginner, intermediate, or advanced.

Places to Visit

Check the Internet (*www.skypub.com* is a good place to start), your local visitor's center, or phone directory for planetariums and science museums near you. Here are a few suggestions:

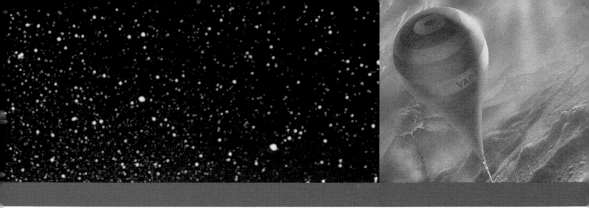

Ames Research Center
Moffett Field, CA 94035
http://www.arc.nasa.gov/
Located near Mountain View and Sunnyvale on the San Francisco
Peninsula, Ames Research Center welcomes visitors. This is the branch
of NASA that sponsored Pioneer Venus and heads the search for extra-
terrestrial life. Drop-in visitors are welcome and admission is free.

Exploratorium
3601 Lyon Street
San Francisco, CA 94123
http://www.exploratorium.edu/
You'll find internationally acclaimed interactive science exhibits,
including astronomy subjects.

Jet Propulsion Laboratory (JPL)
4800 Oak Grove Drive
Pasadena, CA 91109
http://www.jpl.nasa.gov/faq/#tour
JPL is the primary mission center for most NASA planetary missions.
Tours are available once or twice a week by arrangement.

National Air and Space Museum
7th and Independence Ave., S.W.
Washington, DC 20560
http://www.nasm.edu/NASMDOCS/VISIT/
This museum, located on the National Mall west of the Capitol
building, has all kinds of interesting exhibits.

Bold numbers indicate illustrations.

Ray Spangenburg and **Kit Moser** are a husband-and-wife writing team specializing in science and technology. They have written 38 books and more than 100 articles, including a 5-book series on the history of science and a 4-book series on the history of space exploration. As journalists, they covered NASA and related science activities for many years. They have flown on NASA's Kuiper Airborne Observatory, covered stories at the Deep Space Network in the Mojave Desert, and experienced zero-gravity on experimental NASA flights out of NASA Ames Research Center. They live in Carmichael, California, with their two dogs, Mencken (a Sharpei mix) and F. Scott Fitz (a Boston terrier).